SUPPLEMENTARY STUD

for French Horn, Mellophone or E♭ Alto.

To be used with, or to follow any method.

R. M. ENDRESEN

Fingerings for Reference

This chart contains standard fingerings, for French Horn, Mellophone and E♭ Alto. Lower fingerings for French Horn. The upper fingerings are for Mellophone and E♭ Alto. When only one fingering appears it is the same for all three.

1

Majestic

2

Moderato

3

Allegro

S.S. for French Horn, Mellophone and E♭ Alto

4

4

5

S.S. for French Horn, Mellophone and E♭ Alto

6

S.S. for French Horn, Mellophone and E♭ Alto

7

Moderato

8

Allegro

S.S. for French Horn, Mellophone and E♭ Alto

9

10

S.S. for French Horn, Mellophone and E♭ Alto

11

Moderato

12

Scherzando

D. C.

13

Allegro

14

In strict rhythm

S.S. for French Horn, Mellophone and E♭ Alto

15

Moderato

16

Andante sostenuto

17

S.S. for French Horn, Mellophone and E♭ Alto

18

Allegro moderato

19

Moderato

S.S. for French Horn, Mellophone and E♭ Alto

16

20

March time

D. C.

21

Allegretto

S.S. for French Horn, Mellophone and E♭ Alto

22

23

24

25

March tempo

26

27

28

S.S. for French Horn, Mellophone and E♭ Alto

29

30

31

Presto

32

33

34